AF673880

Yahweh Publication

Presents

HARMONIES OF HEARTBEAT

Mrs. Shanmuga Preethi P

Yahweh Publication
Shanmuga Preethi P

Yahweh Publication

Tamilnadu, India

yahweh_publication

Yahweh Publication

yahwehpublication@gmail.com

9363734705

Your words, our passion!

Yahweh Publication proudly presents,

Harmonies of heartbeat.

ISBN: 978-81-987209-4-8.

First edition: August 2025.

Compiled by: Mrs. Shanmuga Preethi P.

Cover design: Yahweh Publication.

Book formatting: Yahweh Publication.

Disclaimer

This book, Harmonies of heartbeat, is a work of fiction. All names, characters and incidents portrayed in this book are either a product of the author's imagination or are used factiously. Any resemblance to actual persons, living or dead, or actual events is purely coincidental.

Every effort has been made to ensure the accuracy and integrity of the material after obtaining the writer's consent. However, the authors and Yahweh Publication declaim any liability for any loss, damage or disruption caused by errors of omissions, whether resulting from negligence, accident or any other cause. Yahweh Publication endeavors to present error-free content, but we do not assume responsibility for any inadvertent mistakes. In cases of plagiarism, sole responsibility lies with the co-authors; the publisher disclaims liability.

This book is a product of Yahweh Publication's dedicated efforts. Yahweh Publication and compilers bear no responsibility for any plagiarized co tent. Only co-authors are accountable in the event of plagiarism. It is important to note that this book does not intend to disrespect any community, caste, religion, creed, nationality or gender.

- *R. Malin Jenifer.*
- *Founder & CEO.*

About the book

Harmony of Heart Beat in the emotional bond of love and friendship creates intimacy and closeness. It is built on trust, understanding, and a feeling of being seen and valued beyond just physical appearance or shared interests. This strong connection can lead to romantic relationships when people fall in love, but it also strengthens friendships. A healthy relationship needs an emotional connection, as it builds trust, intimacy, and stability. This connection helps people feel seen, understood, and valued, leading to lasting and satisfying relationships. Friendships create emotional connections that lead to companionship, respect, and affection without romance. They involve sharing experiences, supporting each other, and creating a safe space where individuals feel valued and recognized. Emotional connections in love are about strong ties that involve romantic feelings, closeness, and a desire for a romantic relationship. This includes a deep sense of understanding and affection, leading to lasting relationships. Different activities can help build emotional connections, such as storytelling, trying new things together, sharing laughter, and showing affection. Also, good communication, active listening, and respecting personal boundaries are important for nurturing these relationships. As a result, everyone has an emotional bond of love and friendship through co-author's writings we only know. Through this, colleagues,

Beloved students, friends of friends, poets, researcher wrote a poem about emotional bond of love and friendship in the harmony of heart beat. Thank you so much for sharing your (co-authors) emotional bond through poems.

Read this book and enjoy. Thank you!

Yahweh Publication
Shanmuga Preethi P

FOUNDER AND CEO OF YAHWEH PUBLICATION

Mrs. R. Malin Jenifer

Mrs. R. Malin Jenifer, daughter of Mr. M. Raja & Mrs. R. Beula and wife of Mr. Martin Manoah. She is a mother of two kids. And, she is an optimistic and energetic person with a big dream from a small town in Ooty. She is a post graduate in Biochemistry and she holds a Diploma in Bio-informatics. Though she is a life science graduate, her interest towards art and literature made her a writer. She has worked as an Online tutor and an assistant professor at different organizations. She is the person who is basically an extrovert and selectively an introvert. She strongly believes in the destination and karma. And, her hope relies on the patience and hard-work. As a follower of Christ, she has a strong belief in a Bible verse *(Phil 4:13)* that says, *'I can do all the things through Christ which strengtheneth me'* and she completely trusts the word and plan of God. She believes that her day starts with the blessings of Christ and ends at his feet. She is a kind of straightforward. She owns a publication unit named 'Yahweh Publication'. She is the person who seeks for the recognition for her work and she believes that this publication is the first step of it. And currently, she is playing roles like writer, compiler and project head under different publications.

She can be contacted through her mail yahwehpublication@gmail.com and her Instagram handle: yahweh_publication.

Compiler

Mrs. Shanmuga Preethi P

Mrs. P. Shanmuga Preethi, is a daughter of Pandi Selvam & Parimala, Wife of Nagarajan, Enthusiastic, Dynamic, Poetess, Writer, Compiler, an Assistant Professor by trade with a Master of Philosophy in English, Master of Arts, Bachelor of Education, Diploma & Advanced Diploma in Communicative and Functional English, Diploma in Gandhian Thought, has been teaching English Language and Literature for Ten years in N.M.S.Sermathai Vasan College For Women, Madurai, have completed NPTEL Course on "Effective Writing", have got Achiever Award for English Literature, author of the book "Unheard Rhythms" under the title "Unsaid Feeling" published in conscience works publication, "Eternal Memories" published in The Little Booktique

Hub, a compiler of 'Identity' anthology published in Words Genix Publication, a compiler of 'Relationship' , a compiler of 'Harmony of Heart Beat' in Yahweh Publication (this anthology) and a co-author of 80 poems, in her point of view Tamil language is her emotion but English Language is her passion, have attended seminars, presented 8 papers, have published nearly 7 Research articles , proceedings with ISBN & ISSN, hobbies are Reading Magazines, blog postings, Articles.

Co-author

Aakaash Chaudhary

A telephone booth, at the edge

Travel to the edge of the world, you will find a telephone booth.
No humans around but a place where cherry blooms in youth.

Feel free to pick up the phone to call your dead and deceased,
Ask them if their life is any better after death, or if it has eased.

For once gather the courage to ask your mother if she's still doing fine.
And ask her if she found someone in heaven to scold to sleep before nine.

Try calling your love and ask, "If there wasn't a death with her will you get another chance?"
Ask if she watches over you, as you stumble through life's dance.

Call that stranger who randomly appeared and gave your life advice.
Ask him for once if he was god or just a human so wise.

Pick up the phone and for once call every soul that you miss or adore.

Let them hear your heartfelt words, your regrets, and
what you implore.

Now you know there's a telephone booth at the edge of
the world.
I hope you pick up the phone and choose me once to
share a word.

\- *Aakaash Chaudhary.*

Co-author

Aamir Raza Khan

Name - Aamir Raza Khan
Age -28
Date of Birth - 26 July 1996
Languages Known - English, Hindi.
Nationality – Indian

दोस्ती

मेरे जीवन के यह तीन अक्षर के शब्द
मेरे दिल के सबसे करीब यह शब्द।
छोटा हो या बड़ी बात
खुशी हो या घम की बात।
उसे शेयर किए बिना नहीं रहना
उसे सोल्व किए बिना नहीं रहना।
मेरे जीवन के सबसे अच्छे पल तभी होते है
जब हम तीनो दोस्त साथ होते हैं।
तब शुरू होती है हर एक बात
एक को दो मिलकर चिढ़ाते है।
पुराने बातों को याद करके हस्ते है
और फिर खुद बोलते है क्या समय था यार,
क्या कहने उस पल के यार।
आज भी मैसेज का इंतज़ार रहता है बस,
फिर क्या? काम छोड़कर टाइम पर तैयार रहना है बस।
कभी गुस्सा तोह कभी खुशी वाला पल होता है
जब भी हमलोग मिलते है,
तोह कभी खट्टी तोह कभी मीठी बातें होती है।
स्कूल वाली बातें से शुरू होती है बात
और कोचिंग वाले बातों पर ख़तम होती हैं बात।
कुछ भी सिक्रेट हो तोह सबसे पहले दोस्त को बताना
किसी को कुछ बताओ या ना बताओ

पर अपने दोस्तो को ज़रूर बताना।
क्या यार है मेरे, यह सारे कभी ना टूटे
चाहे कुछ भी हो, पर यह यारी कभी ना छूटे।
जब दोस्त की कोई बात दूसरों से सुनने को मिलती है
तोह चेहरा उदास कर बोलना,
यह तूने ठीक नहीं किया,
आज से कट्टी है तुझसे,
फिर दूसरे ही पल गले लग कर ,
सबकुछ भुला देना।

- *Aamir Raza Khan.*

Co-author

S. Afrose Jamila

Emotional bond of love

In the garden of my heart, you bloom,
A radiant flower amidst the gloom.
Your laughter, a melody so sweet,
In your embrace, I find retreat.

With every beat, my heart does sing,
For you, my love, are everything.
In your eyes, I see my home,
With you, I'm never alone.

So here's my vow, my love, my friend,
Forever with you, until the end.
In your arms, I've found my place,
Bound by love's eternal grace.

Through valleys low and mountains high,
With you, my love, I'll reach the sky,
Hand in hand, we'll brave the unknown.
Our love a beacon, brightly shown.

So let us cherish each day we share,
In this journey of love beyond compare,
With every breath, my heart beats true.
For in this life, my love, I choose you.

\- *Afrose Jamila.*

Co-author

Ammara Abid

Ammara Abid, is a Mathematician, Writer and Graphics Designer. She wrote many Articles, Afsana, Stories, Poems, Essay, almost on every kind of Urdu Adab. Many of articles published in different newspapers. She also participates on magazines, anthologies and different competitions. Her work is published on different on-line website also include Indian website. She works as a graphics Designer with different foundation. She also works as a co-author in different international anthologies.

Don't be upset

In this crowd of the world,
If we ever lose our way,
Listen! Please don’t be upset.

As we walk side by side,
If one day we drift apart,
Oh my soul! Don’t hold a grudge.

Those gray evenings and fleeting days,
We spent together, hand in hand,
If I forget it all someday,
Listen! Don’t be upset…!

If ever I turn away from you,
And you vanish like a scene,
Just know this, once more,
Please don’t be upset…!

Sometimes think and smile,
At this silly girl
Who left you lonely mid-journey..
But listen!
Never be upset with me…!

I could bear your betrayal,
But your anger drives me mad,

Every moment turns to pain…!
Oh my soul!
I'll accept it all with a smile,
But please don't be upset.

- *Ammara Abid.*

Co-author

Arpit Sarvesh

Arpit Sarvesh, is a resident of Pratapgarh, Uttar Pradesh. At present he is pursuing Masters of Arts in English Literature. He has been writing since 2017.He loves to imagine and write his thoughts in form of words. His first published work is 'Light of Darkness'. He is a co-author of more than 130 anthologies. The themes he used in most of his writings are love-relationship, life and seasons. He got a world record certificate for his writings. His first solo book was 'Words of Arpit'. He compiled a book 'अर्पित की नीति'.

Under a Tree

I saw a good looking girl who stand under a tree,
Has a smile with a good look at me
She is so beautiful than dove,
I think she's suitable for my love
There is many one in that place,
I'm stared at her face
Her eyes is like the eyes of cat,
what I'm looking for may be that
When her eyes blinking looking so cute,
I wanted to talk but she was mute
She wear a traditional dress,
She's is looking the way of mess
I'm very impressed by her behaviour,
If she agreed I'm her saviour
But she was in a some thoughts,
I'm the devotee of my lord's
Her beauty was not defined in word's,
She was a girl who wanted to fly like bird's
God made her for the arpit
I'll declare my love from the pulpit.

\- *Arpit Sarvesh.*

Co-author

K. Ashwini

K. Ashwini, pursuing M.A. in English Literature at N.M.S. Sermathai Vasan College, Madurai. She likes to write her inner thoughts with words and give them life. Love is pure of soul, important, and leads to an emotion. 'Love' does not need a person to give the same feelings back; it's an emotion. It does not need a person in front of us; still, their memories are enough to hold our whole life to live with his or her memories.

EPIC LOVE

Your footprints are everywhere on my shore,
One day! I am afraid that;
The sea waves destroyed your prints,
But, I Am relieved. Because of....
Your memories are in my heart,
Your colors mixed within my dreams,
Your sentiments are still there in my life,
Your joys survived in my mistakes,
I see your screenshots in every single direction,
All my troubles are your live,
And your relationship sleeps in my nobility,
Your fingers in my handkerchief,
My thoughts wake up and you splits from the beautiful love;
The beginning of your life spreading with love!
In my section.

- *Ashwini.*

Co-author

Chenjerai Mhondera

Chenjerai Mhondera is an internationally acclaimed visionary writer, critic, and innovator with over 400 publications across Zimbabwe, South Africa, Cameroon, Nigeria, India, USA, Latin America, and Serbia. A winner of 210+ literary awards, who pioneered the Hi Coup writing form and critiques conventional language and alphabet. As a dissident reporter, editor, and book reviewer, Chenjerai champions social justice and literary innovation, and is a member of various writers' organizations in Africa, India and the world beyond.

Waiting Waiting And Waiting

The wait can't be over
without me waiting for you
Since you left Bulawayo enroute Beitbridge;
Promising to come back
And take care of love mine, all yours!

Since you promised to leave London,
All the way for me.
Since you promised to cancel offers,
To S.A. and cut ties with family
And come wholly to be with

Alone I am collected at the terminus
Of arrival and departure,
Soaring is my temperature,
Temperate not is my desire. I wait.

- *Chenjerai Mhondera.*

Co-author

Dev Srivastava 'Divyam'

Dev Srivastava, was born on 22 May 2005. He is from Gorakhpur district of Uttar Pradesh. His father late Shri Ashok Kumar Srivastava was a travel agent. His mother Mrs. Vimala Ashok Srivastava is an accomplished housewife. Dev writes his full name as Divya Vishok Srivastava which includes the names of both his parents. Dev received his primary education from Lotus Public School in Pipraich, his place of residence. Thereafter, he received his education from ninth to twelfth from Co-operative Inter College. He did his graduation in BSC from IGNOU. He was very fond of reading since childhood and later this hobby took the form of writing. Now writing is not just a hobby for him, it is an integral part of his life. Currently, he is a novelist, poet and Shayar and is taking his writing work towards progress along with teaching. You will also find his works on online platforms like Pratilipi Matrubharti and Wattpad.

Raksha Bandhan

Today's the day, a special bond,
Between brother and sister, beyond.

A thread of silk, a tie so strong,
Binding hearts, where love belongs.

After a year, we sit together,
Brother and sister, in love's weather.

Let me share, a brother's heart,
A sister's gift, a precious art.

Her protection, his utmost care,
He'd sacrifice, without a single snare.

Memories linger, of childhood's past,
When I first held you, so small and vast.

Tears of joy, in my eyes do well,
When you called me "bhaiya" for the first time to tell.

Those mischievous days, I recall,
Pulling your braids, and watching you fall.

School days remembered, laughter and fun,
Midnight cravings, our bond had just begun.

Your wedding day, I held back tears,
For you, my sister, through all the years.

Now a mother, with children of your own,
In my eyes, you're still that little one.

Listening to me, your eyes do gleam,
Our bond remains, a heartfelt dream.

You recall our childhood's every scene,
While I cherish memories, forever serene.

When you'd pull my hair, in playful spite,
I'd smile, knowing it's sisterly love's delight.

When mom scolded you, I'd feel proud,
Seeing you stand, with a heart so loud.

In school, when you'd fight for me,
I'd swell with pride, in pure ecstasy.

Cooking for you, with no end in sight,
Your hunger, my guiding light.

Our fights and quarrels, a love so true,
Our household, with laughter, anew.

Now I see our reflection, in my kids' play,
And let them be, in their own way.

Today's Raksha Bandhan, a promise I make,
In return, I ask, for your heart's sake.

Never look at women, with wrongful eyes,
See only mom, and me, in every surprise.

Your wife aside, respect every woman's place,
A promise, I seek, in this sacred space.

Your lips curve, with a gentle smile,
Eyes moisten, for a little while.

You say, "Sister, I too make a vow,
To stand by you, through life's ebb and flow.

If I'm not there, through thick and thin,
Face challenges, with courage within.

Be strong, and fight, with all your might,
That's my plea, in this Raksha Bandhan's light."

Both made promises, with hearts so true,
And kept them, through trials anew.

- *Dev Srivastava.*

Co-author

Dr. Devanshi Jobanputra

Dr. Devanshi Jobanputra is a dedicated cardio-respiratory physiotherapist, devoted to improving patients' respiratory well-being. With a specialization in facilitating easier breathing, she brings expertise and passion to her practice. Apart from healthcare, Dr. Jobanputra channels her creativity into crafting micro-tales and poetries, offering a unique outlet for expressing thoughts and emotions. Sharing these not only brings her personal satisfaction but also serves as a platform for valuable feedback and insights from a diverse audience.

Experiencing Love

As I watch those tiny eyes watch me stare,
I'm tempted to ask him, 'Can you kiss me?' – Indeed, a great dare !
While our eyes do all the talking,
We no longer require words – the depth of understanding.

Most of the time sweet, at times salty,
Kept growing – at times lovey-dovey at times naughty.
From frustrated lunches to an unexpected dinner date,
Little did we know this collision was our fate.

Crossing of paths, in such a beautiful way,
Our bond grew stronger each passing day.
After all its destiny that brought two souls together,
Our commitment could only make it forever.

The odds of us meeting almost seemed impossible,
A relationship so perfect – felt quite unbelievable.
From strangers to love birds it had been incredible,
Standing by each other's side – we were always so comfortable.

Holding my broken pieces together, never letting me fall apart,
I knew he was the man, who would never break my heart.
From arguments to disagreements to a silly fight,
Always wanted him close to me, hug me tight.

Life wasn't easy, it was a challenging journey,
Uplifting each other's mood, never forgot to say – "I'll be there honey."
Holding hands , promising to always be together,
During good and bad times, we stood by each other.

I hope and pray this relationship works each passing day,
Surviving with the fear of not losing him, this is called 'love' they say.

- *Dr. Devanshi Jobanputra.*

Co-author

Dhawade Gaurav Ashok

The Thread Between Us

A thread unseen, yet strong and true,
Binds me to you in all we do.
Through laughter shared, through silent tears,
We've woven love that spans the years.

In friendship's warmth or love's embrace,
We find our hearts, a sacred space.
No need for words to fill the air,
For in your presence, I'm aware.

The trust we build, the joys we share,
In quiet moments, how we care.
A bond of love, of friendship too,
Forever tied, me unto you.

No storm can break, no time erase,
The ties that hold us in this place.
In every smile, in every sigh,
Our hearts remain, forever nigh.

- *Dhawade Gaurav Ashok.*

Co-author

Dr. Disha Khanna

Dr. Disha Khanna is an erudite researcher and diehard bibliophile. She has a double Doctorate in English Literature and Psycho Neurobics. She holds an experience of two decades in teaching students in higher education. She has been thrice bestowed with Best Researcher's Award and has to her credit more than 90 research papers and book chapters published in indexed high quality national and international journals. She has held various responsible and prestigious positions at a very young age. She has been the Dean of School of Liberal Arts as well as Dean Students' Welfare. Dr. Disha is a certified Trainer from University of Cambridge with TKT Module 1, 2 & 3 along with CLIL and YL. She is also a certified Dale Carnegie Trainer and takes workshops on Soft Skills and other Life Skills related programs. Dr. Disha is also a

Basic NLP Practitioner and takes counseling sessions for all age groups. She is even a certified Reiki Healer and has to her credit many multifarious Art of Living courses like- Happiness course, Advanced Meditation course, DSN, Sahaj Samadhi and VTP. Dr. Disha has an inborn instinct of playing with words and runs her own WordPress Blog titled 'Disha the Phoenix'. She loves pouring her heart out in the form of poetry. She has to credit two anthologies of poems titled 'And Hence the Phoenix Rose' and 'Oneness in Soul Journey'. She also runs her Instagram channel for daily motivational tips and imbibing sound vocabulary @ bombasticvocabulary and establishing deep rooted connection with the world at large. Dr. Disha is also anthropologist by disposition and runs a social service club by the name of PRERNA. Dr. Disha, as her name suggests, is there with a mission to show the right direction to the directionless people and bring smiles on the drooping visages of the youth. She has a strong conviction in the power of Divine energy and stands beholden and eternally grateful to the abundance that she is blessed with in every vista of her life. Dr. Disha is a grounded soul and believes in the mantra of learning, unlearning and relearning.

Impeccable Love of Pondering Hearts

Ultimately awesome duo they have
Impeccably true to oneself
Utterly understanding to one another
Born to rule and shun away all shudders
Pondering beats so intimate
Nailing any type of climate
What anyone says
Least makes them dismay
Fully cognizant about their affair
Crosses all boundaries sans any despair
Theirs is the love of two hearts
That boxes away all the charts
Oneness exists in their journey
Theirs is truly the soul's potpourri.

- *Dr. Disha Khanna.*

Co-author

Divyalakshmani. G

G. Divyalakshmani, from Virudhunagar is a co-author of 11 books. she is studying B.E At Anna University, Trichy. She is fond of reading books. She is more interested in writing poems and essays.

Friends Indeed

There's time for a plant to grow and flowers to bloom.
There's time for people to meet From time to time,
We met new friends Some from near and others far

I'll always be so grateful. For the friends I found! Times that brought us closer. Through our laughter and our tears. Our friendship begins with a seed and how its growing into of trust. loyalty and love

We will share sunshine and rainbows. Sometimes, the rain and the snow We'll stand together through it!
Whenever we gather together.
The Words are not easy to find but love speaks as a common language!

I feel blessed for the friends that I deserve. We're grateful for memories and joyful moment that our crew shares.

It doesn't matter as long as We stay and friendship lasts forever friend who understand your ways. And loves you after all the phases of you

There is nothing like my crown girls.

- *Divyalakshmani. G.*

Co-author

Dixita Parmar

इनका नाम दिक्षिता परमार है। इनका जन्म 20 जुलाई 2003 को हुआ है। ये गुजरात के जामनगर जिले से है। इनके पिता pgvcl के कर्मचारी हैं। इनकी माँ एक कुशल गृहिणी है। इन्होंने अपनी प्रारंभिक शिक्षा अपने गाँव बालंभा से प्राप्त की है। तत्पश्चात इन्होंने शिक्षा जसापर सरकारी स्कूल ओर मोडपर वसुंधरा विद्यालय से की है। 12 सांइस इन्होंने जामनगर में ही ब्रिलिएंट स्कूल ओफ साइस से की है। इन्होंने अपनी ग्रेजुएशन B.Sc nursing की पढ़ाई श्री स्वामीनारायण गुरूकुल से की है। वर्तमान में यह internship और hospital में जॉब करती हैं। इन्हें बचपन से ही पढ़ने का शौक था। यह बचपन से ही अपनी डायरियों में लिखती थीं। इन्होंने लिखने की शुरुआत अपने कॉलेज के दिनों से की थी।

वह तकदीर कहां से लाऊं

पास होकर भी पास नहीं हो,
साथ होकर भी साथ नहीं हो।
दूरियों को मिटा दो अब,
दिल के इतने पास क्यों नहीं हो?
वो तक़दीर कहां से लाऊं,
जिसमें तुम मेरे साथ रहो।
तेरे बिना ये जीवन सूना,
सपनों में भी तेरा ही दूना।
इतनी दूर क्यों हो मुझसे,
चाह कर भी पास नहीं होना?
कहां से वो किस्मत लाऊं,
जिसमें तुम मेरे पास रहो।
तेरे बिना दिल ये धड़के नहीं,
सांसों में भी अब सुकून नहीं।
दिल का दर्द कोई समझे न,
तन्हाई में राहत अब मिले नहीं।
कहां से वो सुकून मैं लाऊं,
जिसमें तुम हर पल मेरे पास रहो।
तेरे बिना तड़प रहा हूं मैं,
तेरे लिए ही जी रहा हूं मैं।
तुम्हें देखूं, यही तमन्ना है,
तेरे बिना ये दिल क्यों मरे मैं?

कैसे मैं दिल को राहत दूं,
जो बस तुझे देखना चाहता है।
तेरे साथ मैं हर लम्हा जीना चाहता हूं,
तेरी बाहों में खुद को खोना चाहता हूं।
किस्मत से ये प्यार मिला है,
अब इसे कैसे छोड़ दूं?
कैसे इन चाहतों को संभालूं,
जब सिर्फ तेरा साथ चाहता हूं।
तेरी आंखों में मैं खो जाता हूं,
तेरे दिल को ही अपना मानता हूं।
तेरी हंसी से मेरे लब खिल जाते हैं,
तेरे बिना मैं टूट सा जाता हूं।
अब बताओ वो तक़दीर कहां से लाऊं,
जिसमें हर दिन तुम्हारे साथ बिताऊं।

- *Dixita Parmar.*

Co-author

Gayathri S

My future Partner

I'm expressing to you in my heart, "you are my love",
No one is able to take you absent mindedly from me,
Because I'm yours! For the sole purpose of mine,
You are my destiny to be born, yet I wish for this,
God dictates our destiny, but you and i are able,
To collaborate together to try and make it are plentiful trustworthy,
Only an honest relationship can be fulfilled in their liking,
If you're aware precisely how much affection I'm showing you,
There is nothing you can do this person could love him,
Considering that he is getting too pleased relating to its,
That's how considerably I definitely and genuinely love you, my sweetheart.
If you wish to do so, my love of my life, I'll always be by alongside you.
The reason is the fact that I'm your gill your lady love,
and I'm the only girl standing nearly you.
If they are standing nearby you,

they either respect your either young or elderly sister.
Purely for me and my love into your heart.
I'm in love with you each minute of each and every day,

a every single second of it.
They were invented to help us express our love;

You are my Remeo; I'm you're Juliet.
It's ignited nearly everything into our world,
Making it virtually impractical for whoever to avert us.
We both are the sole residents in own the universe,
Which renders us crazy and treach erous.
You furnish me pleasant experience, and all I'm faring is enjoying,
The satisfaction in and feeling your love, agony, and one or more of that.
You assure me a relationship is more than just a physical relationship;
That it's a worthwhile and pure kind of affection love,
We cherish our love and the sensation of love it brings.
Through you as the only person are able to experience it.
Obsessed with love, pleased with love in all its forms.
That they incorporate the universe filled with love.

- *Gayathri S.*

Co-author

Ginny Mukesh Jain

Ginny Mukesh Jain, a passionate teen writer, is on a heartfelt journey of literary creation. With a deep love for the written word, she aspires to construct a world of writings that encapsulate her emotions and joys. Her writing endeavors are not only a personal dream but also a way to honor the dreams of my parents. She is dedicated to crafting relatable stories that resonate with readers.

Emotional bond of friendship

It's quite funny how I'm with you
The years seems to all disppear,
The past comes back so clearly
Whenever you're near.
The laughs and the problems
That we managed to grow with,
And whenever I need a reason to smile
I know I can pick out our one memory,
And sit down and laugh like an idiot.
And though I've never said it often
Maybe it was never meant to be,
But am grateful cause still it is.

- *Ginny Mukesh Jain.*

Co-author

Kadambari Gupta

She has done her LL.B. and loves to write poems as it's the best way to express one's feelings and emotions has co -authored several anthologies.

Emotional bond of love and friendship

The bond of love and friendship are,
Special they give meaning to one's life ,
When life pours out problems challenges,
In your cup these bonds make sure that ,
The hot cup poured out does not burn,
Our confidence and faith in almighty ,
So have gratitude in your heart god ,
Made you rich by sending the most,.
Beautiful pristine and positive people,
In your life who made this journey,
An album of memories pleasant and positive.

- *Kadambari Gupta.*

Co-author

Leeladevi Rajapandiyan M

Mrs. M. Leeladevi Rajapandian, MA.M.Phil., likes watching TV, reading books traveling. She is an Assistant professor in the department of English. She is also a NCC Lieutenant for 10 years. She knows few languages such as Tamil, English, Hindi & Malayalam. She is also skilled in DCA, DGT and DTP.

Emotional bond of love

Love is an invisible bond with combining two souls
together.
It is an emotional lifeline. It weaves our hearts together
in a tapestry of love.
Our bond is stronger than the sun.
sweeter than a bird's song.
From my heart to your heart.
From my lips to your lips. I send you a whisper of love
with the names.
It etched in eternal bond.
I knew deep down in my heart that I have found
someone truly special.
The bond we have is unbreakable and irreplaceable.
Being in love with you is the most amazing feeling in the
world.

\- *Leeladevi Rajapandiyan.*

Co-author

Mahima Soni

Mahima Soni is young building writers whose prudence and wit and features her futuristic thought in kindly emotions in young minds. She has written 4 anthologies that mostly deals with felling and intensity of life. She aspires to inspire many young minds.

A friend is an emotional bond, just like friendship love is a human experience.

Friendship and love are two sides of the same coin. When friendship blossoms into love, it's an eternal emotional bond of trust and companions. Love is not a temporary feeling or emotional. Emotional and feelings change, sometimes daily. But true love is everlasting friendships. Friendship is always a sweet responsibility, never an opportunity. Friendship is the purest love. Emotional sympathies just dry up and die us mysterious in friendship as in love. It's relationship like any others. Together we share a bond, even death world violate. Friendship is the only cement that will ever hold the world together. But just friends don't look at each other like that. Your emotional mind is the friendship lead system and the source of happiness, satisfaction, joy, and love.

- *Mahima Soni.*

Co-author

Muskaan

Muskaan is a passionate writer hailing from Bhopal, where she discovered her love for storytelling and poetry. She currently works in the operations sector, seamlessly blending her creative spirit with her organizational skills. Despite her professional commitments, Muskaan dedicates her free time to writing, finding immense joy in crafting both narratives and verses. Her work often reflects the cultural richness of her hometown, adorned with vivid imagery and heartfelt emotions.

The Art of Letting Go

I held you in my hands too tight,
Afraid that if I loosened my grip, you'd take flight.
My fingers, like chains, wrapped around your soul,
Believing that love was control.

I thought love meant staying close,
That in your heart, I'd build a home.
But walls of fear can never be
The foundation of love, it must be free.

I trapped you in the silence of my needs,
In the echo of whispered pleads.
I built cages with words unsaid,
Chained you down when you should have fled.

You were a bird, wings clipped by my fears,
I never saw the weight of your tears.
For I thought love was holding tight,
Not realizing I had stolen your light.

But love, it seems, is not a cage,
It is a garden where souls engage,
Not a prison where we lock hearts away,
But a meadow where both are free to stay.

- *Muskaan.*

Co-author

Nishita Modi

She is looking forward that her words to always inspire her.

She / her

She is not just a she or her,
She is the brighter girl with higher dream's ,
She is the silent girl with a lot of expectations ,
Her dreams are the higher than her height ,
Her kind words says more than any people ,
She want to looking forward and just move on the past ,
She is not any "papa ki pari" , She is Sherni of the world.
Sometime she feel sad but in the next time She react like
a bold girl ,
Her bold acts always inspiring her ,
She is not just a she , She is the champion of the world.

- *Nishita Modi.*

Co-author

Parulalok

Juliet catherine is her second name. She loves writing and drawing.

Heartbeat

Heartbeat is really romantic, and sweet for one I love.

My heartbeat for her only.

My heartbeat is sounded for my girl only.

I love her a lot.

I like the way she dances and do fashion.

She is really talented and good.

I believe she loves me too and I am her heartbeat i feel.

I love my Angela and

she is the best thing in the world.

She is my Angela, heartbeat, love, happiness, success
and priority.

She is my love, romance and life.

I love you my Angela my heartbeat.

- *Parulalok.*

Co-author

Pavithra

She is Pavithra, the founder of the Dreamers Club. And being as a project head, social media handler, admin and jury of Tamil and English language and being as a art and craft, rangoli, cooking, reels jury, community head, manuscript maker, promo head, challenging head, spokesperson, co-operating head, and many more.

Friendship

The bond we had is a joke to you?

Once we were all good.
And now?

Where are you, where are we?

We aren't friends anymore?
Where your promises gone?

- *Pavithra.*

Co-author

Raja Debroy

Raja Debroy is a philosopher, reformer and international writer.

Unbreakable Ties

In the tapestry of life, a thread so fine,
Connects two hearts, a love divine.
A bond so strong, it stands the test,
Of time and space, and life's unrest.

Through laughter and tears, through joy and strife,
This tie remains, a constant life.
A shelter from life's raging storm,
A refuge where love is forever warm.

In moments dark, when fears arise,
This bond shines bright, like a beacon's prize.
A comforting presence, always near,
A gentle touch, that calms all fear.

Through shared memories, and moments dear,
This tie grows strong, year after year.
A friendship forged, in laughter's fire,
A love that's tempered, like a heart's desire.

- *Raja Debroy.*

Co-author

Rangeesh Chandrasekar

Rangeesh Chandrasekar is an MBA Finance and Marketing graduate staying in Bangalore, Karnataka. He is passionate about writing and a great lover of books and articles who has Co Authored and Compiled several anthologies.

Together forever

To all the shining stars and heavenly bodies l am telling,
Of this entire vast universe living,
Good looking flowers and beautiful trees,
Excuse me your attention please.
The bond of love between us is unbreakable, l assure,
However we may quarrel at some time though, being quite sure.
Entitled as loving brother and sister,
Resides as a protector and friend for each other.

Far among the green verdant tall trees,
Owls and pigeons, be aware please,
Ruining our bond and relationship will not give you any benefit,
Every time l am unable to do a work, my brother is there to help and assist,
Valiant, strong and rigid is our partnership,
Earnest, trustful and wonderful is our fellowship,
Robust as a hard rock, elastic as a glue, is our unbreakable bond- will be together forever,
As l am the luckiest one, to get such a wonderful sister.

- *Rangeesh Chandrasekar.*

Co-author

Sanjiv

This is Sanjiv, 13 years old, studying in Mepco Schlenk Matric higher secondary school. He has an interest in writing poem.

Friendship

Friend is important in my life
Friends are our family
There always supports to my favourite way
They not like a knife
Friendship is unbreakable
Friends are always friend
They are running in our mind
Fake Friendship is can be breakable
I will always speak with you
I will never forget him
It is a 6 letter word
but it was always in my world
I have my friends in all time
Friends are my mind
True friend give nice motivation
Fake friends are always pull out bag of them position.

- *Sanjiv.*

Co-author

Saranya Ratna. A

A. Saranya Ratna, currently pursuing an M.A. English Literature in N.M.S. Sermathai Vasan College for Women, Madurai. Her hobbies include reading books and cooking and she believed that reading enhances her knowledge.

For My Long-Distance Friend

Oh, my dear friend,
I'm here waiting for you,
When will you come to see me?
I think about you all the time—
Every day, every minute, every second, my dear friend.
So many things are on my mind,
And I want to share them all with you!
I love you to the core,
And I know you think of me too.
I understand your situation,
But I long to see you, my dear friend.
No one can replace your place in my life,
And I miss you so much.
I thank God for bringing such a precious friend into my life.

- *Saranya Ratna.*

Co-author

Selva Mahalakshmi S

She has completed her UG in B.A. English literature and Diploma in Communicative and functional English at Mangayarkarasi College of Arts and Science for women, Madurai, Tamilnadu. Currently working as an English Language Trainer in Beehive Communication Club (BCC). Recently participate in world record event 'Longest English vocabulary Marathon at Viruthunagar. Trained in calligraphy and good orator. Passionate in writing poems, stories and quotes.

We Three

We three always found together
We are a music, arranged in a perfect rhythm.
We are a clear musical note
When we are blissful.
We are a rap script
When we go crazy.
We are a melody
When we go through hard times.
We are an Epigram
When we give life lessons one another.
We are an Elegy
When we saw one of us in pain.
We are an Ode
When we started to praise one another.
We are an Epic
When we each say our life story.
We are a free verse
When it comes to our friendship.
We started with three
Still we three
Forever we three.

- *Selva Mahalakshmi.*

Co-author

Shinde Subodh

Shinde Subodh Samrat is a dynamic figure in the realm of pharmacy, boasting a Diploma in Pharmacy from Dr. N. J. Paulbudhe College of Pharmacy, Ahmednagar, and currently pursuing his Bachelor's in Pharmacy at Sanjivani College of Pharmaceutical Education and Research, Kopargaon. His literary prowess shines through his authored books, including "The Scientist Who Changed the World," "Pharmacogenetic Personalizing Medicine for Better Patient Outcomes," and "Verses from the Apothecary: Poetic Explorations of Pharmacy and Healing," all available on Amazon. He has also co-authored a few anthologies. Subodh's research contributions, featured in esteemed publications such as the 'International Research Journal of Modernization in Engineering Technology and Science,' reflect his dedication to advancing pharmaceutical science. With a global audience captivated by his insightful pharmacy blogs, Shinde Subodh Samrat continues to make significant strides in shaping the future of healthcare.

Everlasting Bonds: Ode to Friendship

In friendship's garden, blooms a flower rare,
A bond of love, beyond compare.
Through laughter's joy and tears we share,
In heart's embrace, forever there.

Through stormy seas or skies so fair,
Hand in hand, we bravely dare.
In friendship's light, we find solace rare,
A guiding star, always to care.

With whispered secrets, hearts laid bare,
In each other's company, we repair.
Through trials faced, a strength we bear,
For in true friendship, we find our heir.

So let us cherish, this gift so rare,
A treasure bright, beyond compare.
In the tapestry of life we wear,
The thread of friendship, woven with care.

- *Shinde Subodh.*

Co-author

Til Kumari Sharma (Pushpa)

Ms. Til Kumari Sharma as Multi Award Winner in writing from international literary branch is from Bhorle- Hile, Paiyun 7, Parbat, Gandaki, West Nepal. Her parents are Mr. Hari Prasad Basel / Bashyal Sharma (Mayor of Village Assembly) and Mrs. Lila Devi Bhusal/Bashyal. Til is known as Pushpa too. She is Hindu by religion. But she respects all religions. She has published many thousands of poems, some essays, and stories and other literary writings in international magazines, groups and anthologies from (amazon) Russia, America, England, France, Germany, Cuba, Japan, Kosovo, Algeria, South Korea, Argentina, Lebanon, Hong Kong, Greece, Philippines, Hungary, Brazil, Chile, Scotland, Indonesia, Egypt, Serbia,

Tajikistan, Bangladesh, South Africa, Kenya, Nigeria, North Africa, Tunisia, Trinidad and Tobago, Spain, Sweden, India, Nepal and many other countries. She is featured-poet and best-selling co-author too. She is world-renowned poet now. She is poet of World Record Book named HYPERPOEM. She is an international peace ambassador of Bangladesh and ambassador of Moncheri Escapes of India and IACL too. Her real painting is made by Ukeme Udo from Nigeria and digital painting by artist of Cuba (Candido Cuenca). Her World Personality is published in Multi art 8 & 12 magazine from Argentina, biography from Mexico and so on. She is selected in cover page of Asia (Continent) in Humanity Magazine of Russia, Trap Magazine of Egypt and Pachagazine of Kenya.

My Heart Journey

The heart of kindness,
Slow melts in others' pain.
Beating painfully with tears.
Really tearing in failures of love.
Me is sick in that condition.
Seeking medicine to heal.
Then art of words, I collect from mind.
Then heal kindly myself.
The heart is core of life living.
I heal with writing and art.
Me in my sickness, healing with words.
The art of writing makes balance to my heart walking.

\- *Til Kumari Sharma.*

Co-author

Vrushali Gunjal

She, is a heart tethered to the sea, where animals roam and love flourish freely, blooms with sunflowers, and dances through sunsets in the shadow of the stars with the sound of ballad and a decennary period songs.

With "You Only"

"With you only, my essence galvanizes,
In your aura, life's vital force crystallizes.
With you only, existence becomes an odyssey,
As our love conjoins, my soul finds its nirvana.

With you only, I feel the thrum of the cosmos,
A love so transcendent, it rewrites the heart's tropos.
In your gaze, my spirit finds its sanctum,
With you only, I am never bereft of succor.

With you only, our love becomes a legendary blaze,
Illuminating the expanse, our hearts forever praise.
With you only, our love forever resplends."

\- *Vrushali Gunjal.*

Us

Two hearts, a single flame, burning bright and true,
A love that's written in the stars, a cosmic love, forever new.
Our love is a rose in bloom, a sweet and tender embrace,
A gentle whisper in the wind, a soft and sacred space.

In each other's arms, we find our haven and our peace,
A love that's pure, a love that's kind, a love that will forever release.
With every kiss, our love story unfolds,
A tale of two souls, forever entwined, in love's sweet hold.

- *Vrushali Gunjal.*

www.ingramcontent.com/pod-product-compliance
Lightning Source LLC
Chambersburg PA
CBHW062112160726
48282CB00026B/775